When Dreams Aren't Enough: A Collection of Poems About Life

Kyle Switala

Copyright © 2020 Kyle Switala

All rights reserved.

ISBN: 9798635399149

for Joshua Andrew

CONTENT WARNING

When Dreams Aren't Enough is intended to be a work of art. Though its purpose is to entertain, be relatable, and to be enjoyed, the subject areas in the book may offend or effect some, especially those with experience in trauma and mental illness. These subject areas include:

Mature language
Sex
Sexual assault
Sadness
Death

This novel is intended for only a mature audience. Enjoy at your own discretion.

CONTENTS

ACKNOWLEDGEMENTS — i
POEMS

Baby Bird	1
Bright World	2
Twenty-Eighty	3
I'm Me	4
He/She	5
His Castle Will Crumble	6
lovestrong.	8
About Them	9
¡Vida!	10
Fly	11
If Don't You Have Anything Nice to Say, Don't Say Anything At All	12
Too Many Years	13
Just a Good Rhyme	14
I'm Sorry	16
Am I Enough for You?	19
Technicolor	20
I Met a Boy	21
If Jesus Grant You Mercy	22
Don't Fuck This Up	23

Mother Nature	24
Where the Wind Whistles	25
When Dreams Aren't Enough, Part I	26
When Dreams Aren't Enough, Part II	27
My Weeping Eyes	28
The Soloistic Heart	29
The First Day of the Rest of Her Life	30
You're Enough	31
Thankless Achievements	32
Stay the Same	33
Trust	34
The Moth	35
Dance With Me	36
New Roots	37
October 18th	38
The Winter of Her Repentance	39
Love Is	40
Sinking	41
Withering Heights	42
For The Day	43
This Haunted House	44
Life Beyond Now	45

Embers	46
An Unfit Joining	47
The Perpetual Cycle	48
[heart-shaped poem]	49
To Scratch or Not to Scratch	50
Am I Doing This Right?	51
Because it Didn't Happen to Me, Part I	52
Because it Didn't Happen to Me, Part II	54
She Loves Me	55
An Autumn Lament	56
Too Much to Ask?	57
Difference Becomes Us	58
For him.	59
Dear Monty	60
Moonlight	61
Avalanche	62
Beyond These Brick Walls	63
Behind the Wooden Door	64
I'll Be There	65
Smoking Ignorance	66
Until I Met You	67
25 by 25	68
Keep the Fire Ablaze	69

Thankful	70
Containment	71
Calmness in the Night	72
Non-Binary	73
The Sound of Being Whole	74
Comedy and Tragedy	75
All I Want for Christmas is You	76
The Change Among Us	77
Don't Leave	78
Greed	79
The Opposition of Man	80
What Happened?	81
Our Love Will Remain	84
Look at Him Now	85
Inexplicable	86
The Battle	87
The Light Was Still on After the Door Was Closed	88
HAIKU	90

ACKNOWLEDGMENTS

Thank you to the person that truly taught me everything I know about poetry: my senior-year AP English teacher Kelly Armstrong.

Thank you to my mom for keeping the poetry stylings of Dr. Seuss and Shel Silverstein in the house. I think that's where my love of the genre truly started.

POEMS

Baby Bird

Baby Bird is safe
in his Tree of Comfort,
but Baby Bird stares into the future,
wide eyes open to all possibilities.

Baby Bird stands,
his legs strong enough to hold his weight;
his feet planted firmly in the bark,
dirty with memories and mistakes.

Baby Bird bears a battened breath.
He opens his wings,
the winds of a new life whistling his name.

The trees are dark
and unknown.
But Baby Bird is ready to soar.

Bright World

Bright world, wonderous world;
full of color and texture and life.
Birds chirp the air alive
and I. Am. Happy.

Not a care,
but when the sun will interrupt my play.
Not a pain,
but when laying in the dentist chair.

Shopping with mom.
My favorite thing is the popcorn.
And slushies.
And I get to pick out a toy.

Birthday parties are my favorite.
I get remote-controlled cars.
And Legos.
And I'm one year closer to growing up.

Twenty-Eighty

"If only," he said to me,
"Nobody was bossy."
I looked at him awfully.
"I'd have to agree."

"If only," he repeated,
"Nothing was wasted."
"As in cars, you noted?
That sounds splendid."

"If only," he added.
"All the bad was censored."
This is something I pictured.
"If only," I snickered.

"If only these could be,"
I said in plea,
"Whatever do you mean, silly?
You're living in the year twenty-eighty."

I'm Me

I like to play with GI Joes,
but I also play with Polly Pockets.

I'm on a soccer team
(and kick ass on defense),
but I strut around in heels
and I like to draw.

I'm still a kid.
I'm still growing.
And I need love.
And I support.

Does it matter what I like?

If I liked rock music instead of pop
or the color red instead of blue
would I be more of a typical boy?

I know I'm a little different.
I know I'm not conventional.
But I'm me.

He/She

They call me names,
but I don't care.

They taunt me at recess,
but I don't care.

They start rumors,
but I don't care.

I know I'm different and that scares people.
Maybe they're afraid of what I'll say next,
or maybe they're jealous that I'm me.

I stick with my friends
and that's all that matters.
They care about me
and I care about them.

When they laugh at me,
it doesn't matter.

When they stare at me,
it doesn't matter.

When they call me names,
it doesn't matter.

His Castle Will Crumble

A young boy rides that board
like an eagle soaring through the sky.
He stabs the buttons of his PlayStation 2 remote.
He plays with his trains and action figures,
for he does not know pain.
He does not know maliciousness.
Yet.

His castle will crumble from that faithless day in the basement,
when he sees things that he never thought he'd see.
when he is touched in ways he never thought he'd be.
At least this young.

This boy is all too caring.
This boy can only see the good in the world.
His eyes might be blinded,
but only by the bright light of wonder and caring hands.
He is not weak, but he is not strong.
He is only a boy.

Monsters, on the other bloody hand, only take.
Some only care for themselves and what they want.
Wandering roads are paved with intentions
only fit for those that shouldn't be allowed to walk them.

This was not the first time.
And it won't be the last.

His innocence was taken that day.
Along with years of sanity and privacy.
And his mother's heart.

lovestrong.

lovestrong.

Not just love.
Not just strong.
Anymore.

More like hard.
Or depressing.
Or heart.
More like life.
Or broken.
Or pain.

Pain.
Pain.
All I feel is pain.
Pain is in everything.
Pain is in life.
It's in touch.
It's in thoughts.
It's in emotions.

Emotions.
Emotions are hard to read.
Hard.
Strong.

I used to be lovestrong.
Now… Now I'm just… heart broken.

About Them

Their hair flows like an ocean of perfectly beautiful waves.
Every day I wait to see what they look like,
to see if they look as good as previously.

Wondering.
Waiting.
Staring.
Deciding.
For them to notice me.

The wait is killing my inner soul;
killing it like my cat does to a spider.

Wondering.
Waiting.
Staring.
Deciding.
That I'm complete with them.

As complete as a half circle.
The cap spins on the table as I spin thoughts in my head.
About them.

¡Vida!

Vida.
La buena.
La mala.
La bonita.
La feo.

Todos vivimos.
Esta vida loca.
Gracias, Ricky Martin.
Es dificil. Es triste.
Pero vivo, lo que hacemos.
Felicito a los que optan por mantener sus vidas.
Mantener la calma y continuar.

Queremos ser conquistadores Espanoles,
pero no podemos.
¡Esta el conquistador de tu propias vida!

Fly

I need him.
Like a kick needs a drum.
Like up needs down.
Like a summer rose needs rain.

I sat, hunched, by my window;
waiting.
A little animal flew up;
whistling.
"Forever and always."
"But wait… how long is always?"
Then he left
and I chased.

I chased for five months,
but it ended.
It ended like it started.
Like falling.
Like a text message.
Like a joining of two unfamiliar hearts.

He landed. Nestled.
In the arms of another man.
Not confirmed, but I know.
That has to be why;
why he flew in the first place.

If Don't Have Anything Nice to Say, Don't Say Anything at All

Pain is in our minds,
but our bodies can't think.
Who's to say the soul can't hurt?

Does the girl hurt when daddy calls her fat?
Does the boy hurt when the jock calls him a fag?
Words are as physical as knives
and weapons don't belong in ignorant hands.

Too Many Years

Why am I thinking of him?
7 years later and my head is fuzzy.
My heart is in knots
and my stomach churns in a storm of hurt.

Maybe it's not him.
Maybe it's the thought of him.
Maybe it's the romance novel.
Maybe it's the love songs.

Why do I let myself feel this way?
I have the option of care-free and happy,
but I choose the painful thoughts
and hurtful moments.

I've had others,
but I need someone else.
I need a clearer head.
I need a stronger heart.

Just a Good Rhyme

The carelessness of guys,
competing to catch the eyes
of the people they like.

Making the ones that like them stabbed,
deep with the spike.
The spike of regret.
The spike of envy.

But every time that happens we don't forget;
making us all tremble,
some even start a bet.

What can I do to prank the crusher,
so mean they can be.

Burr.
The thought of it all
makes a shiver down the spine.

Into the oven of relationship,
baking the bread of love;
thoughts stuck in my head.
They all think they're above

Smoking the way I am;
hurting what I do.

The pain of it all.
Sometimes I just want it to stop;
stress makes me ball.
Using me like a prop
for the enjoyment of humor.
Making me hate,
wishing they had a tumor.

I felt like being evil.
Don't shun;
I'm not a bad guy.
It just has a good rhyme.

I'm Sorry

I'm sorry...
That I couldn't be enough for you.
That I couldn't love you the way he does.
Even if that love is shared six times a fucking week, like
rabbits on Valentine's Day.

I'm sorry that your heart has moved on.
U-Hauled out of town to find another Nashville, Tennessee
with some other love history.
History in the making.
History is an art,
painting the walls of my heart
with the most crimson of blood and pain.

You couldn't even think of splashing that white love that
rendered us hopeless for each other;
Un-dying affection around every corner.
Though the same thought crosses my mind as much as music
across Stereo highway.

If Christina Aguilera could pull us back together,
I would cross oceans and rivers of ACTs,
just to be able to pencil you through that mirror.
Mirrors give us all reflections,
but what you can't see is me with you.

Through make-up applications and applied earrings,
I hear your name - piercing the reflective glass,
like an underpaid Claire's sales associate.

What you'll hear from me isn't what you'd expect.
You'd expect I'd give up hope, lose all humanity.
I'm not a hermit on the street
begging and begging just for the mention of your name,
though that's what I feel inside.

No.

What you'll hear from me is a testament to how much my
love burns for you like the grease left on the gas-burning
stove from grandma's homemade meals of my childhood.
She cares for him just as much as I care for you,
though you don't see it behind your lust-stained eyes.
It's always there for you to reach out and take it.

Do your fingers fit perfectly between the spaces of his?
Does your heart ignite a feeling of passion and fire when his
match comes around?
Does he love your beautiful, compassionate soul when it
comes down to the fact of the matter?

I love you like a back-alley hooker loves crack.
I will not give up.
I will not give in.

I'm not about to be some little brat, crying all the way to the
bank, just because my boss touched me.
I will take that stance, that mistreatment.
I will stand tall as he finger-fucks the sustenance out of my
heart and takes advantage of my every crevice.
I will not falter until I stand tall with you
in my arms.

In the cold, dead winter,
while everyone sits warm in front of the fire place,
sipping hot chocolate and telling stories of their childhood,
I'll be there.
Waiting.

Second chances are for those strong enough to withstand life.
For those that don't want another path to take, for fear it will lead them over a waterfall.
Second chances are for those that are truly meant to be.

I'm sorry I let you off that fighter in the sky of reliability,
while you plummeted towards the Earth and pulled that parachute reading "Scott."

I'm sorry I couldn't be all that you wanted me to be.

People change like the seasons.
And this boy will melt the snow at the drop of an amber tinted leaf of forgiveness.

Live and let go.

Could you bare to let go of me?
I can't do the same to you.

Am I Enough for You?

How are you supposed to love someone
When they're just a flea in your hair?
I-
I'm sorry.

I said I wouldn't hurt you
and you said you wouldn't hurt me,
but words tend to get caught
in webs of lies and deceit.

Technicolor

I wish my life was in technicolor.
Instead, I'm immersed in black.
And white.
Absence of life.
Absence of love. Hate. Compassion.

Is it not but everyone living in greyscale?
The eternal darkness.
We aren't Marilyn Monroe.
We aren't James Cagney.
Or anyone in between.

How can one experience life,
when hiding in the shadows,
under great stress,
and kept from the three-dimensional world of adventure?
Maybe one should live by one's words.
Then one would live life like life should be lived.
I wish my life was in technicolor.
Instead, I'm here.
Writing this.

I Met a Boy

I met a boy…
with a heart of gold;
and nimble fingers;
and luscious lips;
and the determination
of a thousand wounded men.

I met a boy…
whose timid smile
lights up a room;
whose amber eyes
are dripping with wonder;
whose heart-filled laugh
makes me smile from ear to ear.

I met a boy…
who won't take no for an answer;
or back down from a fight;
or let me do anything for him;
or tell me when I can help.

I met a boy…
that I love beyond belief;
that also loves me.

I met a boy…
and it was the best thing to ever happen to me.

If Jesus Grant You Mercy

As darkness floods you over
and you begin to beg and plead and weep.
If Jesus grant you mercy
for just one last night of sleep.

Although you've done no wrong,
that's how you see it in your mind,
the one that's crying in her pillow
won't find it just as kind.

The relationship between you two
was supposed to be forever.
But now you and her
shall always live endeavored.

I hope you never rest,
as abominations like you do.
She shall surely, in all her years,
never, ever forgive you.

Don't Fuck This Up

Don't fuck this up.
You have a tendency for irrationality,
so don't fuck this up.

Take it slow.
Dot your I's and cross your T's
and don't fuck this up.

Put in the work,
take the time,
and don't fuck this up.

Establish a connection,
build trust,
and don't fuck this up.

Most importantly:
don't fuck this up.

Mother Nature

A house is only as strong as its foundation
and trees only take root in fertile soil,
avoiding rocks and going as deep as they can.

The wind tries, but will always fail at knocking the sky scraper down.
There's a reason mountains and hills don't move.
Instead, they roll.

Though roads prove useful,
the bridge is far more versatile.
What else provides passage over and under?
But never through?

Birds can only fly so high.
Cheetahs can only run so far.
Man can only destroy so much.
Right?

Where the Wind Whistles

Where the wind whistles,
beneath the snow
and the cracking trees,
there is a place that my heart calls home.

Where lions and tigers and bulldogs roar
and cherries put the season in motion.
Where hops is the main export
and lakes are more like oceans.

Amongst the sweaty sneezes,
I found true love and true friends.
I spent hours cleaning the burnt popcorn
and earning (not much) money I could spend.

I almost packed my nest and flew away.
Iron bars almost restrained me from my life.
I swerved home when I shouldn't have
and never went back in strife.

When I've strayed,
I've realized there's no place like home.
Some move away,
but only if it's on loan.

Life is a bit slower here.
This beautiful place is special, you see.
The people are kind and courteous.
I doubt anyone will disagree.

When Dreams Aren't Enough, Part I

When dreams aren't enough,
and life sets in,
you realize what is and isn't,
and you start to grow up.

When dreams aren't enough,
they are reality.
Reality is having a roof.
Reality is a full stomach.

When dreams aren't enough,
neither is anyone else.
You can't always rely on others,
but you can rely on yourself.

When dreams aren't enough,
they're child's play.
You can't touch dreams.
You can't make money off dreams.

When dreams aren't enough,
nothing else is.
Beyond how far dreams get us
there is a vast field of regret.

When dreams aren't enough
what else is there?

When Dreams Aren't Enough, Part II

When dreams aren't enough
and reality sets in,
I'll be there
To wipe away your sin.

When dreams aren't enough
and when life gets too hard,
make me your dealer.
I'll pick the right card.

When dreams aren't enough
and your head is heavy,
bring me your storm.
I'll be your levy.

When dreams aren't enough
and you can't carry on,
don't worry, my dear.
For you, I'll run the marathon.

When dreams aren't enough
and your world comes crashing down,
call on me
and you'll wear my crown.

My Weeping Eyes

Does he know I love him more
than the wind loves the rain?
than the grass loves the sun?
than the night loves the moon?

I try to tell him,
but efforts fall short.
Time slips away.
Be dry my weeping eyes.

The Soloistic Heart

The castle he builds crumbles under his feet.
There's nothing but his hope to hold him now.
45 years have come and gone
with nothing to show but bruises and lies.

This life he's built will be his demise;
his mistakes are all he has to hold.
Wickedness will always be a downfall.
Karma is merciless to the unapologetic.

Would he have been more empathetic,
perhaps helped those in need,
instead of pleasing his own soul,
he'd be living a fulfilled life.

The universe tends to reward those that live in strife;
those that think of others before themselves.
Egotism has no place in the utopian society
and the soloistic heart beats an unrewarded ballad.

The First Day of the Rest of Her Life

Beneath the arch she cries,
for she knows in her heart
this is it.
This is what she's waited for.

Years, she spent chasing dreams,
forcing her square peg into round holes,
only to have them be triangles.
Deceit has never fooled her.

But the day is finally here;
the day she cries over raised glasses,
declaring her love in front of family
and she couldn't be happier.

You're Enough

When you don't think you're attractive,
I do.
When you don't think you can do it,
I do.

When you can't carry the burden,
I can.
When you can't see inside yourself,
I can.

When you wonder why I love you,
I don't.
When you think you're not cool enough,
I don't.

When you don't think anyone's there,
I am.
When you aren't apt to please yourself,
I am.

When you can't steady your breathing,
I will.
When you don't believe in yourself,
I always will.

Thankless Achievements

Cast in gold,
because knowledge is priceless,
and forged from all-nighters.

The blood, sweat, and tears
make the gem shine.

Achievements compacted into one vessel,
because the measure of worth is in jewelry.

Twelve years of work
and waking up far too early
for a fucking piece of paper
and a ring?

Stay the Same

Will this feeling ever fade?
The constant craving your kisses;
wanting to wrap you in a warm hug;
the security of having you around?

Do the "firsts" mean any less
as we get older?
Will I still adore everything you do?
Is there a point at which this all becomes mundane?

What about when we have a house?
And kids?
What then?
Will you still feel the same?
Will I?

I hope contentness never pervades my soul.
I hope that you always want for me.
I hope-
No.
I know
that every day the only thing I will think about
is returning home to you.

Trust

Skin to skin
and heart to heart.
alone in this room,
may we never part.

Your touch mirrors mine.
We kiss in the moonlight.
The sheets cover our insecurities.
I never want you out of my sight.

There were days that I wandered;
I was lost, without a soul to call mine,
but then you jumped into my life
and the universe gave me the biggest sign.

"He is perfect for you."
"He'll solve everything."
Lying here, I believe you did.
I just need to accept everything you bring.

The Moth

Moths collect on the stone wall.
What do they hide from?
The winds must tear them from their thoughts.
Is this a normal fall occurrence?

Does a wandering moth ever find home?
Their wings flap for purpose,
but what purpose is that?
Do they know not what they fly for?

They don't sit and wonder what they are,
where they'll go
or what they're doing.

The moth travels to and froe with knowledge;
knowledge of its past travels
that it grows from.
That's all it cares for.

Dance With Me

Dance with me.
Let me see your worries fade away.
With every step you take towards me
I feel as if you'll stay.

Dance with me.
You'll come to see.
Watch time fade away.
Don't be afraid.
Take my hand
and I will lead away the day

Trust in me.
Take a chance.
Feel the Mambo.
Do the dance.

New Roots

Basking in the morning glow,
she breathes in lavender
and exhales worry
and never again will she be contained
by the afternoon shade that plagues her
and she's as free as pollen in the wind,
ready to plant herself
in the most fertile of soil
and build herself a new life
among the many different plants
and she's ready to be among the birds
and the other animals
that will take her to new places
and teach her new ways of growing;
of spreading her leaves
and knowing
what her seeds can really do
and she's ready,
oh, is she ready,
to grow
and touch the sky
and be taller than the weeds that surround her.
She's ready for her full bloom.

October 18th

Imperfection is perfection.
Who needs a perfect date?
Spill your water on me.
Have an allergic reaction.
The time we spend together is perfect enough.

The Winter of Her Repentance

Baby deer is fawndling in the brush.
Mom doesn't give up yet.
Winter is coming.

She will protect her youth at any cost.
The wolves are hungry,
but she doesn't budge.

The blanket of snow calms the fields.
Silence dances around them,
toying with their every will.

She does not hear the footsteps
of the monster on its mission.
It's too late to look back now.

Love is

Love is being able to share anything.
Love is gazing eyes,
thankful that eyes are gazing back.
Love is knowing you're safe.
Love is picturing a future
and working tirelessly to make it reality.
Love is a gentle touch at the perfect time.
Love is finding a soul mate.

Sinking

A fisherman lost at sea
doesn't wail around his worries.
But when the tide rises,
he's the first to abandon ship.

Withering Heights

You're my normalcy.
You're my new routine.
Take my past life and hit delete.
I don't mind.

Rewrite this story.
Take out the chapters of loneliness,
the character arcs involving pain,
and the fog-filled setting.

Instead,
paint landscapes of happiness,
create climaxes of nothing but love,
and a resolution that would rival even Jane Austen.

For The Day

Since I saw you,
I believed in love at first sight,
but you told me, "No"
and I said, "Okay, that's fine."

Then fate brought us together
and I called it a sign.
You walked in, I chose you,
and you fell for my lines.

The universe brings two people together,
no matter what they say.
I knew when I saw you
that we'd be together on this day.

So when I say, "I love you,"
I mean for the rest of our days.
When I say, "I want you,"
know that'll never change.

As much as we argue,
we'll always feel the same.
I love you
with all the blood in my veins.

This Haunted House

This haunted house has been hollowed,
ravaged by pain and destruction
and self-depreciating ghosts.

Loneliness plagues these decrepit halls,
while once-lively rooms sit vacant.
This Haunted House is a home no more.

Life Beyond Now

Does the future hold a picket fence
or life on the 24th floor?
Will my students learn from me?
Will I still be entertaining?

I can so clearly see him,
with his chestnut hair and amber eyes,
basking in the glow of the fireplace,
as we dress the tree in twinkling beauty.

But do I see a little Monty,
wonder in his eyes, dimples on his cheeks,
as he discovers what's been hidden?
Will our future be as bright as this?

Embers

14 years have come and gone
and what is there to show for it?
Houses and cars don't mean much
when a fire is waiting to start.

An Unfit Joining

Blind is the infatuated eye
to all things selfish.

Guarded by insecurity,
the wholesome heart, that once was,
turns on its previously astute owner.

"In love" doesn't necessarily mean "whole";
the opposite can be true.
What is a tarnished shell
can remain ravaged,
if the cause is a soul
who is battered and bruised himself.

The Perpetual Cycle

The days get longer.
The drinks get stronger.
I'm not any less tired
and life isn't any easier.

the heart
fragile yet strong
easily broken but passionate
taken for granted and guarded for life
it's the strangest thing that we listen to it
we give someone the key and they take it
unrestricted access to our feelings and
our emotions and our sanity
a smile can melt it away
a glance can worry
life will never
be the same
a heart
beats

To Scratch or Not to Scratch

To be a cat,
not ravaged by bills
or work stress.
When your only concern is protecting your house
from the bug on the wall.

Having food available at every hour
and endless toys at my disposal
would be a nice change of pace.

Sure, there would be loud machines to run from
or plastic bags to hide from,
but there's always the couch to retreat under
or the cabinets to perch on.

Yeah, living the feline life wouldn't be so bad,
until your owner abandons you.

Am I Doing This Right?

How do you show someone you care?
Is saying "I love you" enough?
Actions speak louder than words.
His actions scream.
Mine whisper.
Bad relationships are the epitome of one-sided conversations.
Will what I say ever be enough?

Because it Didn't Happen to Me, Part I

I never believed it could happen,
because it didn't happen to me.
Now my eyes are open;
now I can finally see.

Doubt fills your mind
and life looks bleak
when things that take people hours
take you a week.

Some get married
and some have babies,
while I sit around,
not holding any degrees.

I was a painter among doctors,
my brush guiding my life.
They sailed through Harvard,
life at the will of their knife.

I realized everyone's life is their own.
We all move at a different pace.
Each person has a different track
and we each are at a different place.

Once I knew this,
my path, I began to treasure.
I opened up my heart

and everything came together.

That's when I found my way
and finally realized what I wanted.
I finally fell into my own;
I felt like my life counted.

And that's when I met him.
Like a board finds a dart,
we were instantly connected
and now he'll forever hold my heart.

And that's when I found happiness.
The dog found its owner.
This heartless fool
finally found a donor.

Now my eyes are open;
now I can finally see.
I never believed it could happen,
Because it didn't happen to me.

Because it Didn't Happen to Me, Part II

It's taken some time,
but he's finally gotten there.
There have been countless misguided paths
that have all lead to this one.

His journey is just beginning,
though this isn't where it started.
He is a fawn beginning to walk;
fumbling his way through life.

Even if he's years late,
and his token is behind the others
in this board game we call life,
he has arrived.

And he's right where he should be.

She Loves Me

She loves me.
I love her.
I'll take her hand;
Our love can't be bigger.

I love her.
She loves me.
Were first to each other;
That is key.

There are special things that attract us;
We hold on to each other's words.
Our love is free,
Like beautiful white birds.

We have our ups,
We have our downs,
But we always work it out.
Never will we frown.

We may lie,
We may be hurt,
But the one thing I can count on,
Is my love with her.

An Autumn Lament

The first sip of coffee passes my lips,
Steeping the night away.
The crisp air tickles my nose.
I wonder if apples are in season yet.

The leaves sing their siren song of autumn,
pumpkins shout from porches,
and the cold bites my ankles.

Too Much to Ask?

I want Christmas dinners around the farmhouse table.
I want embarrassing singing on the way to drop the kids off at school.
I want late-night discussions over glasses of wine and happiness.
I want glances across the room that lead to bouts of laughter.

I want united families enjoying each-other's company.
I want held hands walking down the street and never letting go.
I want entwined fingers watching the sun disappear.
I want sleepy eyes under a blanket, basking in the heat of the fireplace.

I want smirks shot across the kitchen as Monty says something inappropriate.
I want your smell to invade my car.
I want endless nights of laying on your chest and you on mine.
I want your every essence to become mine.

Is that too much to ask?

Difference Becomes Us

Normalcy is the oppression of creativity.
Uniqueness is plagued by labels.

Gay isn't unique.
Feminist isn't unique.
Cop isn't unique.

Ironic,
that in efforts to normalize
and
in our dying desire to label all,
we've sucked the creativity out.

Those that are different become normal;
something that we try to avoid,
at all costs.

For him.

I will do better.
I will be the man that only exists in your dreams.
I will be your knight in shining armor.
No.
I will be the queen to your king;
always at your side,
ready to take a knife to the chest for you.

I will show you the love you deserve;
the love that you've wanted,
but that nobody has ever given you.
I will hold your heart between my palms
and cradle it until it breathes again.

I will learn from my mistakes.
I will take each moment,
dissect it,
and use each morsel to better myself.
For you.

Dear Monty

Dear Monty,

I hope you are born into a judgmental world
that's littered with liars and deceit.
I hope Bobby steals your Hot Wheels
and you cry for days.
I hope you fall off your bike
and skin your knee.
I hope you experience infidelity with your first love
and feel heartbreak like nothing else in this world.
I hope you fail an exam.
Or two.
I hope you lose your job
and live paycheck to paycheck.

I don't wish you an easy life.
I don't wish you a simple life.
I wish you a life full of pain, hardships, and loss,
because I know it will only make you stronger.

You will not just survive.
You will thrive.
You will look life in the cold eyes and say, "Fuck you."

Moonlight

Coyotes cry in the pale moonlight.
Crickets sing their siren song.
The grass hides the truth.

The rain rids the worry,
collecting in a pond of memories

And I.
I'm left wondering:
How will the night end?

Avalanche

Pouring yourself over work
until nothing in life matters more.
Every conversation becomes a distraction
and everything never mattered less.

Masochism is an art form.
Balancing just enough sleep to function
and adrenaline from accomplishments
is delicately walking a tightrope without a net.

As beautiful as the first snowflake
and as destructive as an avalanche,
this natural disaster will eventually swallow sanity
until reality is just a dream.

Beyond These Brick Walls

Complexity is the keystone of life.

If everything was simple,
life would be a box of a house
with little architectural interest.

A mansion is far more exciting.

With archways of stress
opening to vast rooms of accomplishment,
where floors are never dull.

And multitasking is painted across the walls.

Behind the Wooden Door

Beyond the leaves tinted with pain,
past the pond littered with regret,
down the path ravaged with disgust,
there lives a sturdy house.

In this house resides a woman.
She bakes all day and crochets all night,
for she hasn't a clue what lies behind the wooden door.
She knows her place in this world.

I'll Be There

As the crow flies,
As the wolf howls,
As the duck quacks,
I'll be there.

As the glass breaks,
As the wind blows,
As the earth shakes,
I'll be there.

As the ear hears,
As the voice cracks,
As the eyes see,
I'll be there.

Smoking Ignorance

Cigarettes make me sick,
but the smell of harsh opinions hangs heavily in the air.
Hearts have homes
and a lion is no friend to the cage.

Life is a delicate thing.
Delicate to touch.
To hold.
To feel.
Delicate doesn't know pain.
Pain is all but an acquaintance to conversation,
woven between laughter and criticism.

Who are we to judge the moth that is drawn to the lamp,
for it doesn't know anything but.

Ears listen, eyes see, but lips don't part to words.
Instead
unintelligence, and uninformed accusations cloud the air.

Unenrichment.
Unenlightenment.
Unforgivement.

Until I Met You

I'm not sure I knew what life was,
until I met you.

Late nights at the bar
and insisting on Netflix
has nothing on holding you
and dinner dates.

25 by 25

25 by 25
And I'm not done.
A collection growing faster than a child.

"You better enjoy it, 'cause it'll be over before you know it."

There's too much blank space.
I must fill it.

My body is a museum.
I have the real estate,
why not display masterpieces?
There isn't even an entrance fee.
The whole world can admire it.
But first, I must finish it.

Keep the Fire Ablaze

I fear complacency.
"Lackluster" has never been in my vocabulary
and never will be.
Such a fear can't be the embers
of a failed relationship.

Thankful

Thankful for my friends,
that they always make me laugh.
Thankful for my family,
that they don't judge.
Thankful for a roof over my head,
that I always have somewhere to return.
Thankful for my health,
that I could be far worse off.
Thankful for my job,
that I enjoy and am good at.
Thankful for my love,
that he completes me.

Containment

How does anyone not talk about these feelings?
All I want to do is shout from the rooftops.
I want the world to know:
he's the one.

He can't escape my thoughts.
I hope someone asks about him (and I),
just so his name is mentioned.
Restraint is hard.

Calmness in the Night

The moon holds secrets in its enticing grasp.
Staring into it,
behind fluttered clouds,
I got a glimpse of what's real.

Waves of emotion can be blinding at times.
The light cast from this lonesome being
can calm any tide.

Non-Binary

The world is not black and white;
it exists wholly in multicolor.
So why would everything that exists in it
be so binary?
Who are you to assume so?

The car doesn't only
travel left or right.

Morning and night
aren't the only times of day.
In-between exists a myriad
of colors, temperatures, and life.

The plane doesn't only
go up and down.

The rainbow, even,
isn't solely stagnant colors;
they blend and meld,
causing a beautiful phenomenon.

If the world was, in fact, black and white,
it'd be dull.
There'd be no flare, no spark.
no me.
Who wants a world like that?

The Sound of Being Whole

You came into my life at the perfect time.
I used to spend my days wallowing,
relying on the bottle to keep me company.
I guess I got used to the quiet.

But then you wandered in,
filling my life with the most beautiful noise.
What once was a solo concert
is now a thirty-piece orchestra.

Comedy and Tragedy

Step out.

The heat from the lights
awakens my insides with a shock of adrenaline.
It's hot, but there's no changing that.
These clothes must remain.

Breathe in.
The first look at the statues is always the most frightening.
But it does pass,
as fast as it comes.

Speak every word intentionally.
Make every pace meaningful.
Don't break character.

Before I know it,
it's over.
While in the process,
I want to run away.
I want to quit.
When it's over, I'm sad it's over.

And I can't wait to do it again.

All I Want for Christmas is You

We share a passionate kiss
as the wind whips our hair in our faces.
The snow hasn't fallen yet,
but the world is quiet, as if it has.

Our love is as strong as the day we met.
It will never fade or falter.
Seeing you brings the same joy that Christmas morning does.
You will forever be my holiday cheer.

The ribbon has nothing on my love,
tied up for you.
But now the snow falls delicately,
like I did for you.

As much as I wish,
as much as I write,
nothing could make me happier,
than Santa putting you under my tree.

The Change Among Us

The wind streaks the snow across the pavement,
as if the Earth is preparing to give birth
to a beautiful baby named Winter
or bulking up to take the gold
in a body-building competition in cold.

It's here to stay.
The solemn mistress whispers
her depressing song in my ear.
Get ready for bitter nights
and craving the heat.

As everything else does,
this will eventually fade.
The gray skies will break to the smell of lilies
and sun that thaws the bones.
The grass will grow
and life can start again.

Don't Leave

He kisses me like he's never kissed another
and will never again.
Our lips form a perfect mold,
locked forever, the other holding the key.

Though his departure forms a hole
that only he can fill,
I know he will again,
so I wait.

His light will return to this darkened room
and I will be whole again.

Greed

We take life for granted,
wasting minutes at the hand of a bottle
or needle.
Save nothing for those that don't.

The Opposition of Man

We smile and we frown.
We laugh and we cry.
We think and we talk.
We scream and we whisper.

We ride and we drive.
We fly and we crawl.
We run and we walk.
We soar and we stop.

We love and we hate.
We work and we play.
We dance and we sit.
We sing and we sleep.

We rise and we fall.
We stand and we kneel.
We grow and we shrink.
We live and we die.

What Happened?

When you're young
you're told,
"don't judge a book by its cover."
Your teacher,
your parents,
your youth group leader;
they all say the same thing,
"don't judge a book by its cover."

When you're a child,
eyes full of hope and wonder,
you abide by this.
You might initially think this ideal
pertains to literary work;
in which case,
the point is kind of moot.
Am I going to choose the book with the picture of the
seductive vampire or George Washington on the front?

As a child,
you don't see color.
You don't see sex.
You don't see wrinkles around eyes
from decades of third shift
or a finger
that is just a little too big to put a ring on.

So what happened?

How did we go from
"sure you can be my best friend,"
to
"back away from the Range Rover"?

What animosity stomped out our light,
so our eyes cannot see what our heart does?

How are we so blind
to only see the world through a microscopic lens?

The woman that you take slow and small,
yet impeccably meaningful,
steps away from
in line at McDonald's -
with hunched shoulders and ragged clothes -
is just trying to get her only meal of the day
with the one dollar and seventy-two cents
that she sat in the sub-zero temperatures
for six hours to get.

The man incoherently mumbling on the bus,
who you raise an eyebrow at,
only wishes he was able to stare at his wife
a few seconds more,
before seeing semi headlights
just outside her driver-side window.

That girl in the corner of your class,
that doesn't have any friends
and doesn't talk to anyone,
is trying to heal the emotional and physical scars

that have been left from night after drunken night
of her father slipping in-between her thighs.

How did we get to this point?

In a ravaged world that is crying out
for our affection,
how can we focus on the number of our waist
or how many zeros follow a dollar sign
on the tag of a purse?

In a world that's run by the number one
on the Billboard Hot 100,
how can we ignore what's between our ears?

Who determined beauty is more important than knowledge
and that it's the most impartial standard?

I wish we trusted our hearts
as much as we trust our eyes.

Our Love Will Remain

The birds are flying back,
the sun is shining through,
the snow is melting away,
and I still have you.

Concrete may crack,
asphalt will do the same.
Waves destroy the bay,
but our love will remain.

Viruses will attack,
climate change will be
something for which we'll pay,
yet, you'll still have me.

Look at Him Now

Look at him now.

He's not a shy child anymore.
Instead of running from strangers,
he embraces them.
He doesn't just have dreams anymore,
he lives them.

He's taken a dull life
and turned it around.
He's become more than he ever thought he could;
done more than he ever thought he would.

He couldn't be more proud.

Inexplicable

How does a word define an emotion?
All that is can't be summed
in four letters.
One syllable.

It's something that's experienced, not discussed.
It's not for a pen and paper;
but for wide eyes and a rapid heart.

It's a perfectly placed head on a chest,
rising and falling with each breath,
the tides of compassion waning.

It's him consuming all my thoughts,
hoping he's asked about,
just so his name is mentioned.

It's picturing a future,
with a farmhouse and kids,
and tirelessly making it reality.

It isn't the words on a page
or pronouncing admiration to another.
It's something felt from within;
Intense to experience and impossible to explain.

The Battle

When I have to leave you
my heart leaves my chest.
My body runs off memories
until the next time you're in my arms.

When we don't see each other
the withdrawal sets in.
My blood runs hot
and I wait for that quick fix.

When we spend the night apart
the bed is far too cold.
My side means nothing without yours
being occupied.

When we are joined as one –
that's the day I'll feel complete.
My heart and my head
will finally be at peace.

The Light Was Still on After the Door Was Closed

Though he's learned so much,
there is plenty more to learn.
He's only a portion through.
Hopefully.

His story is only half-written;
his painting halfway done;
his game half-complete;
his dinner half-cooked.

Nobody knows where he'll end
or what will happen.
But it doesn't matter.
It's his path to take.

HAIKU

The pool is still full
But crunchy leaves have fallen
Has summer left yet?

Children are like eggs
They need constant attention
Or they will spoil

Crows cry as they fly
With the force of a bullet
Don't care where they go

The leaves begin to crisp
Cool wind whistles the air alive
Fall is here to stay

Shoes on the pavement
Like tiny ants marching along
Where will they end up?

ABOUT THE AUTHOR

Kyle Switala lives in Fenton, Michigan with his darling cat Louie. He's earned a bachelor's degree in psychology and is currently pursuing a master's degree in education (with a secondary teaching certificate) from the University of Michigan – Flint. He also has a license in cosmetology and still works as a hairstylist. When he's not working or doing school work, he's watching something on Netflix or writing. Writing has been a passion of his since childhood. This is Kyle's third work of publication, his first two being fictional, young adult novels called *Elite* and *Superhuman*.